CONFESSIONAL

poems by

Fletch Fletcher

Finishing Line Press
Georgetown, Kentucky

CONFESSIONAL

Copyright © 2024 by Fletch Fletcher
ISBN 979-8-88838-684-2 First Edition
All rights reserved under International and Pan-American Copyright Conventions. No part of this book may be reproduced in any manner whatsoever without written permission from the publisher, except in the case of brief quotations embodied in critical articles and reviews.

ACKNOWLEDGMENTS

I am very grateful to the editors of the following journals who did me the honor of publishing
poems from this collection:

Phantom Kangaroo
"Confession #174"

Peregrine
"Confession #19"

ARTS by the People
"Before Confession #835"
"Leave Confession #835 Alone"
"Not Confession #835"
"Please, Leave Confession 835"

Publisher: Leah Huete de Maines
Editor: Christen Kincaid
Cover Art: Tanya Voytus
Author Photo: Gabriel Gutierrez
Cover Design: Elizabeth Maines McCleavy

Order online: www.finishinglinepress.com
also available on amazon.com

Author inquiries and mail orders:
Finishing Line Press
PO Box 1626
Georgetown, Kentucky 40324
USA

Contents

Confession #0: Law of Confession 1
Confession #1: Freudian 2
Confession #2: Make Believe 3
Confession #6: Most Blood 4
Confession #608 Box in the Driveway.. 5
Confession #4: Discovering Frater pugnatus... 7
Confession #9: Sins and the Father 8
Confession #19... 9
Confession #22: Birthday Call from Grandma's House............................ 10
Confession #18: Away from the Guggenheim 12
Confession #358: I actually want to be a father 13
Confession #347: Learning Fatherhood from Silence 15
Not Confession #835.. 17
Confession #100: Questions and Lies 18
Confession #23.. 19
Confession #164: Ode to the Book Spine..20
Confession #108: Uitwaaien..21
Confession #591: Unrequited 22
Confession #701: What we could be.. 23
Confession #105: Wish to be Music... 24
Confession #252: Waiting.. 25
Please, Not Confession #835 27
Confession #62: Afraid to Feel... 28
Confession #583: Give Me.. 29
Confession #479: Ashamed... 30
Confession #163: I used her.. 31
Confession #269: Poem with a Mouth on its Dick.................................... 32
Confession #99: Never had I ever.. 33
Confession #36: No Woman... 34

Confession #37: No Woman 35
Confession #42: Orchard Street 36
Before Confession #835 39
Confession #13: September 40
Confession #213: The Big Rock 41
Confession #196: Olean at Eleven 42
Confession #299: Length of Memory 43
Confession #05/17 44
Confession #7: Godless 45
After Confession #835 46
Confession #52: Another Drink, Please 47
Confession #95: Party 48
Confession #122: Socially Anxious 49
Confession #173: Urge 51
Confession #174: Fear 52
Confession #175: Honesty 53
Confession #333: Rationalized 54
Confession #8 55
Confession #463: God of Hunger 56
Confession #756: Tempered 57
Confession #20 58
Leave Confession #835 Alone 59
Confession #726: Emotions and Men 60
Confession #660: As a Man 61
Confession #661: As a Man 62
Confession #662: As a Man 63
Confession #663: As a Man 64
Confession #664: As a Man 65
Confession #79: Response 66
Confession #80: How to be a Man 67
Confession #418: Define a Man 68
Confession #800: Tell me where it hurts 70

Still Not Confession #835	71
Confession #423: Ode to Me	72
Confession #50: Debit	73
Confession #3: Beaten	74
Confession #567 How to Talk to a Liberal (if you must)	76
Confession #01/17	77
Confession #02/17	78
Confession #5/24: Student Accommodations	79
Confession #221: Reading News	81
Confession #5/28: What they are lying about	82
Confession #835	83
Confession #-1	84

Confession #0:
Law of Confession

Like another zeroth law it must be true
first that confession is an energy before you
can understand how laws work
how Einstein proved light can make this massive
how there is no way to destroy them

so I marked and measured and buried mine
let them seep slowly
Fukushima to my ocean

nobody will know
what's dying.

Confession #1:
Freudian

I hate my mother in no unordinary ways
I hate my mother for having me in a world this hard
I hate my mother for the world being this hard
I hate my mother for giving just a little less love than I think I needed
I hate my mother when I feel my face so empty of scars I remember
    the texture of all the trees she kept me from all the fears she sat me down
    to recite like our only religion
I hate my mother when I feel my side for the fossils of dog teeth or my skull
    for the tip of an iron or my collar for this kneeling bone she couldn't
    save me from
I hate my mother when I want to cry and hate myself for having a penis
    and hate that *all men are assholes and all men are stupid* and I hate
    that I cry anyway
I hate my mother since she called me *an experiment* and kept true to the trial
    and error until she found a child even I know is my better
I hate my mother since she called me *lazy* and I refused to keep fighting
    because I was tired because I was depressed
I hate my mother since I told her *I'm better. We don't need the therapist.* and
    she let me win that one
I hate my mother because I am more her than myself some days
I hate my mother in all the ways we laugh about "hating" family around our
    friends, in all the ways "I hate my mother" is more a code than anything.
I hate my mother because I grew old, and hate is easier than fear, is more
    acceptable than fear, is something I can say as a joke and not let on
    how scared I am
I hate my mother because I grew old in every open eye but hers
I hate my mother because I can't live anymore only in her eyes

Confession #2:
Make Believe

I destroy everything I see
as I drive, picture my hand
against a highway lamp
as if my perspective were truth,
grip the glossy silver post
between my thumb and index finger,
pluck it from the roadside as if it were a drought-shriveled daisy.

I throw the light like a pub dart
into an oncoming car. The windshield
shreds like taut tissue. The driver
ends like rotten fruit. The asphalt
gives like sand as the tide rolls out.

And I never think about the lives ending, because
they aren't real. They don't have faces before the dying daisy
hits them. There are no families
waiting off in this world I imagined
they tried to return to, to hold, to apologize for
breaking those mugs in the sink or those pictures
in anger. They can die over and over again
because their worlds are so far from mine. They can die
because I still get to work every morning,
home every evening,
and when I sleep I see no faces
drawn in shadow on my walls,
behind my eyelids, in the other worlds
I make to live in.

**Confession #6:
Most Blood**
> *For Shannon*

I have held your hand
in every hospital
from the day you were born.

    And there have been too many.

The laugh comes from the blood,
how you lost all of yours
before you could walk, how you pump a dozen strangers
through your heart a day,
how you are always cold
from so little life in your veins, but
it boils over before the hat could even consider dropping.

Before you burn yourself
to frozen blues, remember First
Sister,
I carry our blood for both of us.

**Confession #608:
Box in the Driveway**

I know my sister
woke up in blue. I'm pretty sure

she was the one
on the floor crushing cardboard,
plastic, the doll tied to the shredding
package, deftly stripped naked, bent
until the legs expelled. And I'm pretty sure
my sister tossed them.

She was the one clawing the presents
with her squealing teeth, rending
the cards, the box everything
came in, the driveway
between bed and breakfast
our father
snuck across.
Gravel and exhaust.

Our father
snuck across the driveway while we slept.
A box of goodbyes from his trunk dropped
by the road's edge
to the farthest coast of our country.
His handprints
washed away by mist
under the quarter moon.

I'm pretty sure I stood
silently stolid. My feet were sculpted
one half-step apart. The screaming
lashed all in front of me. The tears
slammed all in front of me. I remember
I arose so like stone. And I am

pretty sure my sister cursed, popping
snot bubbles with shotgun wails.

I'm pretty sure my mother
welled up only when my sister
let loose. Blond haired whips,
switching cabinet doors. Her nightgown
knees hitting tile. Sparks
by the cold stove.

All the fire a girl can be
she was, alight everywhere, scorching
her own ground. I appeared
more the unused stove.

Mom saw me shrugging,
shifting in my marbled skin.

I remember her hand fixed to my
sister's back, between sharpened blades.
I know she rocked my sister, dulcetly. Wiped her
smooth, blue cheeks.

Confession #4:
Discovering Frater prognatus

The difference between
half-sister and *sister* is seven
genetic markers or several
seconds of a still heart
when a cleat connects with her
face and she's saving a goal and you flash
every rainbow hue of panic and rage,
storm the field toward a referee
who forgot what the whistle was.

The distinction between
cousin and *brother* is found after
two splits of a karyotype or a series
of nightmare-filled weeks where sleep
brings new ways he dies overseas and you find it
difficult to attend a farewell fling
if it means it's all real.

An easier classification is between
father and *dad*
as they require a shot of sperm
or twenty years of being there,
always being there,
respectively.

**Confession #9:
Sins and the Father**

Bless me father for I have sinned.
Though this is not a Catholic father, no
matter the parallels of their presence:

the way they both exist
in the aether, in the clouds, just behind them
in the broken sunbeams you trace and know
the clouds are just a flimsy curtain:

the way neither broke
silence as I learned the impotence of prayer, the dull ache
of kneeling, how pressing palms and squeezing
fists always end as empty hands:

the way I was blessed most
with the lack of them. But here,
in this space of white
that is my confessional

I know I seek the blessings
of biology, deeply. Help me
exorcise this need for blood
to be better than my witness bore.
Dear God, let me lose Him or
absolve me of His sins.

Confession #19:
>*for Ryan*

When his fake was taken and tossed on the table
with a curt *goodbye*, I knew the smoke would crawl into his lungs
as he stoked the anger with American Spirits.

We talked about anger a few weeks after, understanding
people paint emotions with only the primaries:
sad, mad, glad.

Maybe if we had the words for feeling the way we do
for color, we wouldn't see ourselves as paint-by-number, but
as Pollack meets Picasso, splatter cubism, the kind of art I would at least admit to
misunderstanding.

Instead we storm down Duval Street
looking at the shops and the drunken smiles through the red tip of the lighter
and tell ourselves we are this one shade
and maybe if we pull enough black into our lungs we can close our eyes
and the world will be dark enough to sleep
without crying.

Confession #22:
Birthday Call from Grandma's House

His tone was almost pitiable. All
I heard was a stranger,   afraid
of his son.   A choked-up stammer
15 years of stories
I don't have time to learn.   I don't have time
to work up the fire in my blood
          burn him
from my skin.   All my anger
          for a stranger. I wish
          him a happy birthday
and he says my name
like a confessional prayer.
The whispered warble of his voice
some fraction guilt, some portion penance, some sorrow
for being caught. The plastic of the receiver
feels like a wooden lattice, flimsy
divider for words,
that still keeps his face
blurred as each question and joke
sounds more and more like *Hail Mary*.
Which sins caught in his throat? Which
waving syllable of *hello* brought
my jaw-line into his room, made my body
seven, made his body out of bending knees?
I'd not thought myself on this
side of God without wrath in my tongue.
How can I yell at a grown man's ghost?

The moon clung there when I took breath,
and I no more know its touch than his.
         Or maybe
I was born on a new moon.   Maybe
the sky itself waned
         in my lungs and absence
surfeited my first taste of life.
                          Or maybe,
just maybe, his life and   mine
                          aren't connected.

I can wish him a happy birthday. The rain can spray California. I can breathe deep tomorrow's morning, feel nothing on the ride home.

Confession #18:
Away from the Guggenheim
For Tanner

It was some time between Pollock's
Enchanted Forest and the burnt rubber
air of Fish House Road
we ran out of words in the grey
coupe you helped me find
between your lacrosse practice
and picking a college

I found a few words
rattling in the console
knew of a couple of phrases
in the glove compartment
meant for emergencies
something Mom made me
put in my back pocket
even she was too afraid to use

The radio didn't work day one
so eventually we rehashed the oldies
together ourselves
the best from when you were young
all the ones we knew by heart and nothing
from this year left our lips
or touched our ears

Confession #358:
I actually want to be a father

I.
This black stains
scratches   white sheets   scores it
bold   impudent   mocking in its inked perch
before me   a scar
seen on the wrong side of my   skin   There
is no breathing this heavy
air   with such weak lungs   they can't
dare   disturb
              the stillness.

II.
Thumbs on a screen, haptic
feedback, every touch the same
pressure on the pads   whorls deltas
only the slight stretch of the tendons   tells
difference between   want and rejection.

I can't feel the weight
of leaving
like this the way I say   *I can't*
repeats so often   I can't
tell   if telling her   I can't
continue is telling   me   *I can't*
or   *I won't*
or   *I shouldn't*
send something of   myself
a step further than   myself
than my grave
then this cycle   *I can't*
                  break.

III.
I know I am a coward in this, in these
clothes,   these words
I will not utter
or the edges of the wire,   barbed and bound
around the strangled sound   will tear

tears from me in rents and trenches
shaking afraid
by the blood I could bring
I might be   him
or
maybe I'm afraid   I won't
                        I can't
maybe I'll stay
and all the good he did
        through his absence
will prove to me that my line is meant to die
childless   or see the ruin a life could be
when incapable hands refuse to release.

Confession # 347
Learning Fatherhood from Silence

Biology

I am the shadow
of an absent father,
opposite and still
immaterial.
For so many miles separate,
I can't make a turn
without negotiating your statue,
your memorial, the look of the bald spot
on the back of your head
since I can't remember your face.

And sometimes
I want to cry
when I turn off the lights
and think how much I must resemble you
standing in the dark.

Choice
Dad occupies the couch, the corner two-seater,
back to his bedroom door,

reclined in the end spot, line of sight for every first
step inside. It's night, probably 1 or 2.

TV's playing some movie nearly mute.
Everyone's asleep—even Dad. But he can't go to bed

until I'm safe and he knows it. I tap him on the shoulder.
He flutters awake, arms still crossed like he doesn't want anyone

to put another chore list, another bill, or a seventy-first hour
of work on his open chest. I nod and whisper,

Night, Dad. Turning to descend the stairs to the couch
that is now my bed, I hear the recliner clicked closed,

the TV silenced as the room blackens
with no star's gleam. I reach the comfort

of three cushions and a sheet as Dad latches his door
the floor above me, finds his way to Mom in his sleep.

Not Confession #835

This place has four waterfall walls.
Rivers flow from all six cardinal directions they spit
themselves back into their bodies. The center,
Halley teaches, has the stars in circle pirouettes
about each other. This is less a place
than a trout. More a grizzly and I am
the trout ever jumping for the left-front tooth, except
there are no confessions in fins like I bring to bury
in the ratites' flightless feathers. I tell you
I am lonely,
and you are not shocked. I whisper
here, knelt to the coyote's ear,
I know why I deserve it
and still you are not shocked.

Confession #100:
Questions and Lies

Does a confession need a tear, need an ache
in the gut as it is pulled from the scar-tissue used
for a coffin, or can I confess a feather on a breeze, or
the breeze itself, or
the way a friend looks at a feather
on a breeze and my confession is as much that
I saw them looking as it is how light my bones feel
when I am with these air-hunters, these sun singers, these liars
who sometimes remind me confession and storytelling are both true
to the soul if not always
to the tongue.

Confession #23

Milk and Honey applied
directly
to the ears and eyes and
lingering on the tongue as it tastes
lips of another
should be enough to know the world
is not hopeless so long as you share
small prosperities.

Confession #164:
Ode to the Book Spine
> *for Darla Himeles*

Bravery as glue and pulp and grip
all the black spatter
you solid spreading triumph of completion you
herald of the everready thought I see you
cracked hear your ecstasy moan delicate
fingers peel you apart in her
hand she snapped you
both shivered like lovers holding
everything you needed

your words
her eyes

Confession #108:
Uitwaaien

    for the Crew and Roman's

Muscle as breath
bent knee   breeze
around a pillar
    between concrete faces

glass doors   eyes without direction

and the tunnel is running
    escaping   pushing a breath to a gale

into other lungs

into days or years from now

two hundred or thousand miles

and there   maybe
you'll be

and I'll breathe again

**Confession #591:
Unrequited**

There is a spark with you
but I am hydrogen
a Hindenburg
sideways shot
hazel eyes brought
immolation
a dozen times two and times
again I didn't know
ashes could be made of ashes perhaps it's masochism
perhaps it's punishment
but damn you
burn so good

Confession #701:
What we could be

It could be a touch like water
rain under full view of a midday sun
coolly at the crest of the neck
the lips perk a bloomed rose

or like a saltless sea
breathing over sand to hold the beach
retreating when the moon calls, but
always holding the land

or it could be the river.
No, not the river.
Not the water racing to be something else
touching the land half like a scar and
if it stays, if it moves itself up the shores
for rest
devastation
and salt
added in drops.

Confession #105:
Wish to be Music

What if I broke into song, into sound,
into progressions of Major and Minor G,
a deep blue major seventh
played together with diminished ninths
and then the sound the sky made
when it first saw the ocean fill itself
drop by drop and stopped feeling
alone? What would I sound like?
Would you listen to me?

Confession #252:
Waiting

Did you notice the shark hanging
above the doorway when you entered
not mounted
not stuffed
just sort of suspended there
swimming through the air
teeth like raindrops like
ice sickles just waiting to fall but
this shark isn't a man-eater
exactly
more of a taste tester
just sort of nibbling
every passerby
every time they step
through the threshold a little bit
taken from the shoulder
a morsel from the tip of the nose
maybe something of the hairs on the back of your neck
shaved a little bit by the bottom teeth
as you scrape by him
or her
I'm not sure
how to sex a shark
that floats above us
sits behind us

I've heard they always have to keep
moving and I question sometimes
if it's a different shark above every door or
maybe it's the same one as always
moving to and from teeth
waiting to pick a little bit
more of me everywhere I go

I'm wondering maybe this time she'll take
my whole head maybe this time
I'm going to have a little bit more of me
lost than I can possibly live without

I'm wondering this time
is it going to still be a shark or
is it going to be a person
is it going to be the hand of someone I knew
is it going to smell a little bit like lavender
like the body wash
like the hairspray I knew one time in my teens
a lot of times in my teens
is it going to be something different or
will it always be teeth

Please, Not Confession #835

Please,
kiss the open lips of this
lie and leave
before the end.

I drew monsters
in margins to keep
truths I need to love

truths I need to love
me.

truths I refuse
to map.

Please,
do not get close
to my edges.

There be dragons here
afraid of their own fire.

**Confession #62:
Afraid to Feel**

By the paisley drapes, I sipped malbec
from a clear plastic cup and half-listened
to half-a-dozen conversations
crammed into the tiny hotel room.

Bodies filled the beds, the chairs, the floor
from bathroom to window and all the faces
were friends. Giddily, she asked me,
the way you would in middle school
when crushes were scandals
and feelings were open targets,
about a crush she thought she saw
in my smile.

I looked her in the eyes and denied,
that way you would in middle school
when rejection was homicide and admission
was chicken on the tracks,
and she left to laugh
with other friends, leaving the lie
naked between us.

**Confession #583:
Give Me**

It is selfish to want love
like an infant

coat every wall with wailing
until it is touched
until the world comes to it

solve emptiness with fingers
                              and lips
                                          and arms
meant to touch
                but mine
mine flail
in the night air

grab only ghosts of shadows
dreams of memories
                      of when the air was warm
                              with lover's breath

all the sadness and fear sought some other
refuge since my arms were full
                      and content
                              and this is me

                        wailing

this is me
open-armed
demanding of the world to give me
                        give me
                              give me

        because I am scared
        and the world is dark
        and I am so very empty

Confession #479:
Ashamed

In my starting months the brown-haired boy with the pentagram
pendant atop his plaid shirt warned me
where to stand to stop the secret
smiles and whispers:
Hallelujah

I swear I didn't want distractions, so I stayed
in my slightly longer suit, stood
where I could control
the way the room looked
while checking homework to hold off
stares.

Some part of myself I hate
liking where they chose to rest their eyes.

Confession #163:
I used her

I had her because I could
obviously

the way she looked at me in classes
that half-shy, half-bold, not quite meeting
evenly in the middle

the way she laughed
a touch too long at my jokes

the way she glanced slightly
too quickly at the door when I walked in

the way her seat moved one closer
one closer
one closer
until she was sitting almost on my lap

and I was lonely
and I didn't think much further than
I could have her
I could be less lonely

I could hope she would be more interesting
later
more beautiful
later
more fun
later

but for then
for those days
I just wanted somebody
and she said yes
and later
never happened

Confession #269:
Poem with a Mouth on its Dick
>*after Sosha Pinson*

My left hand was clenched at my side. The right
was open, palm pressed softly to the smooth, black,
back of her head.

I had already decided I was done with her   —bored—
before she stood in the doorway and I forced
passionate kisses.

My fingers knew to glide from the collar to
just behind her ear. The heel of my other hand touched
every piece of cloth from her shoulder to thigh.

I figured I would try asking   —taking—
for once, but I could not let myself
speak.

I had only one word left for her,
but it could wait
until morning.

Confession #99:
Never had I ever

We confessed by silently drinking.
Six of us, a fire, and a cooler
less and less full of beer
my whiskey disappearing in swigs
after smirking questions about sex
about us
about if we had ever.

Goddamnit
I wish I had had more to drink that night
I wish I had to drink more that night

and I smiled at her every time we didn't drink
and she smiled at me every time we did

and when the game had ended
I leaned in to press my booze-drenched lips to hers
still grinning a little
proud a little ashamed
a little interested in how many more drinks we might take
next time.

Confession #36:
No Woman

I will not lie, not now.
There never was a woman; never
a woman dressed in summer
green to match only her left eye. I never knew
pressure of her breast on my chest,
chill of her fingertips
lain across my abs with the light
cresting dawn through ruffled eggshell drapes.
If I had known –
If there had been –
I would not be able to stand
in all the empty spaces she should be.

Confession #37:
No Woman

I can't help but lie. This is what love is: lying
mostly to yourself,
mostly.

I can still taste all the women I've loved
if I bite my top lip.

Not all the women
I've kissed.

Their tastes and scents and even
some of the faces came clean from me.

I press and scrape the soft red skin sometimes
when it hurts living outside of memory, but the flavor's running low

I can't find more anywhere.

**Confession #42:
Orchard Street**

I must have taken that left turn before
Cono's Autobody six times a week
for four years. Today I have fresh coffee
in one hand, my favorite
micro-ball pen in the other,
and I feel the wheels
spitting the grit of long-gone winters.
I close my eyes and the headlights lean
into that first curve,
automatic, to meet you.

        The first corner house slides
        by the right, that white one
        with only the sides facing streets
        freshly painted. The other two
        chunked and ripped by weather.
        In the backyard, the youngest boy
        lost his foot to the lawn-mower at five.
        I can't imagine being his older brother
        pushing the blades
        behind a muted blue fence,
        no neighbor's home to hear.

                Take the left at *Pine,*
                I used to think was *Dogwood,*
                to where we broke-down for twenty minutes.
                Five months at most after I kissed you
                we rounded that bend
                ten minutes before midnight curfew
                and the T-Bird coughed
                grinding metal as the exhaust
                dropped on the pavement.
                Only six minutes to stroll to your bed,
                but you waited for my Grandfather
                and tow-cables that made you late.
                We joked about my junker on its trunk

          by moonlight and coming-spring breezes,
          laughed how I never disappoint to make mistakes
          adventures. I held you when the wind picked up.

     Two rights past muffler's grooves
     I cruise *Birch*, a quarter-mile
     to the bright red conversion van
     with ladders on the roof
     and *K-9 Search & Rescue* stickers
     slapped on the back doors.
     Your father's "fair" Dutch accent mangled words
     to a song I don't recognize
     over the kabobs grilling on the deck.

One of my favorite pictures was captured there.
Your earrings were bronze,
silver and leather
dangling from your right lobe
sweeping the tip of exposed clavicle.
Your hair wrapped back to fill in the gap
between sparkling metal and satin
skin of your neck. Your temple tilted
touching my black-and-white bandana.
I wore the yellow soccer jersey
from the summer team of the snapshot.

          I played a game that day
          you came to see with a blanket,
          book, and water-bottle set at the half.
          A third bout of blindness smashed me
          while I defended the eighteen.
          The next week I had an MRI,
          told the doctor details,
          all three incidents occurred with you,
          though for two we both breathed heavily.
          Luckily for me my sight came back
          each time to freckles
          dotting beads of sweat around your nose,

blue-green eyes unwavering as hazel glass,
auburn hair mussed indoors or shimmering
shades I can't discern
in the afternoon sun.
I remember the taste of those subtle, pink lips
four years since I lost them.

        I cover a pang above my left floating rib
        whenever I see my T-Bird
        dead in Mom and Dad's driveway,
        a pang on the right when I wear that jersey
        from the team, scattered and forgotten.
        One stabs my throat
        when I drive past that left turn
        before the autobody shop
        and have no call to follow it.

But I don't want this to be sad.
I don't want to cry
from loss or loneliness.
Look at all the travel of my pen
at the thought of your face.
It's beautiful.
If I cry at all it will be because it is

Before Confession #835

Do you count the birthdays of secrets,
memorialize and idealize their flailing
youth, their rebellious adolescence, the slow march
into middle age
where they settle into your skin
like routine
and wait to die?

Do you know the orbit of secrets, the time
it takes them to see every shining side
of you, the speed at which they sow and reap
and hunker down for the long cold that comes
with biting winds?

Do you remember how you felt
when your skin was open sky,
untilled plains,
clean and free
of headstones?

**Confession #13:
September**

I hate my birthday. I buried it
at 11 when I counted my friends
on half of a hand and stopped understanding
how seeing this particular side of the sun again
made any sense to celebrate.

Take the shovel to the boy,
to the earth,
to the way things decay.

Screw the stars.
Let them sit above
paint whatever pictures they damn-well please and leave me
to murder myself
every year, celebrate
with all the solemnity of the morning after
a wake.

Let the years become snakeskin, let them
be tulips, let them
be rows of our yesterdays longing to be
cut down.

Keep whatever bits of body, whatever
few scraps of flesh might be redeemed or
at least
reused.
Pay no attention to the man
grave robbing.

Confession #213:
The Big Rock

It was a mountain the way a tub is
the ocean when you're five and clouds can be caught
if you climb high enough. It was a mountain
with my flag on its peak, sprawled across it
watching boats and swords and three-eared rabbits swim
from the edge of the woods to the point of the roofs.
Standing atop it I could look down on David
as he skateboarded by with all his huge
fifth-grade friends. I could see over my mother's head,
into my father's eyes, evenly, and jump
from the top of my little world to the grass with barely a shock or jolt.
Decades later the mountain is moved. I see a small stone,
white and gray, a grave marker for the fallen giant, or
maybe it is a goodbye note. Maybe
if I run my hands along its grooves I can read
which part of the sky my old friend has traveled to, but
I don't speak stone like I did
when I was five.

Confession #196:
Olean at Eleven

Ivory pair tipped in ash. Skin
thin and loose on knuckles of the hand that set
wax to cloth pairing stained whites. A thousand spiders
blackened a porch wall. I found the fire
atop another. I did not know
they were pure for death.

Confession #299:
Length of Memory

Do the children still hang
over the rivers tracing eyelashes, counting down
wishes between dawn and dusk? Are the alchemists
still turning violins into birthmarks, still finding
patterns in the skin of unused
pathways to Heaven? Is Death still
sad? Do you even know
what I am asking?
I'm asking if it has been forever: that space
between the beginning
before it began
and the time too far after the end.
Everything happens in forever. My mother's pelvis
cracked for me in forever. It made me
a shadow in the corner of my grandmother's
attic that moves when nobody sees it.
It made me a shadow
unstitched to boots.
It made you
a memory inside this shadow,
the dream of shade forever.

Confession #5/17
> *For Esther Louise*

I want to miss you more
Pick a chair in every cafe, not quite a corner,
in the back by the window and
empty it.

Call your smile to the emptied space,
chant until the warmth of your words hold
midwinter air at bay, invoke your spirit to fill us
as it always did.

But this is just me. I only see the hole of you
in poetry, in community, in this part of me I live
by choice.

I barely know the edge of your pull.
How deep in the black must your family be? How empty,
how heavy, how terrible to lose the sun of you?

I want to weep for them more,
but like the death of anything in the heavens
the wound in the night can be forgotten.

How do I keep the scar in my sky
from closing?

Confession #7:
Godless

Bless me father for I have sinned
by omission of you. Not rejection, though
I am told the road to Hell is paved
with unbent knees, and these,
these walk with an ache, but not for the celestial,
not for the seraphim songs or touch
of supplication. Oh, God,
I call your name as a hollow word
because light is just a piece of the spectrum
to me. I see miracles in dust and feel them
in the gentle press of atmosphere on my shoulders.
I see no hand. Divinity is thoughtless
to me. Oh, God. I simply do not know
if there is a You out there
among the missing bits.

After Confession #835

First you lose your fingerpaint
      then the fingers
           the songs
                  the way the sky seemed so tall
                        and the ground wasn't whispering your name.

Confession #52:
Another Drink, Please
> *For Morgan*

I don't really know when to stop
especially when the drink gives me something to do
with my hands
and the group stirs in what could be ecstasy,
though I can't tell,
and I stand a safe few feet behind but
even when my eyes are all that see me
I know the onlookers are uncomfortable.

**Confession #95:
Party**

There are too many bodies
that are not me. There are too many
mouths that have tasted lips
I only imagine. Why can't
all eyes be mine? Why can't my eyes
know a fraction of what the rest decode?
I see light
half as well as anyone else.
I see the eyes glance my way and know
that is the extent of words. I know
so many things that are at best
wrong, at worst
lies I tell myself
to never change.
Can the night be me forever
seeing through new eyes?
Can the night be forever me
knowing this time in the dark
that life can be more
until the libations fail
and the old reality becomes my walls?

Confession #122:
Socially Anxious

Rhythm shoes and two score heels can't
plant on the tile dance floor. I know this scene,
these smiles, this decibel of loose delight.
Toward a corner or two
clusters of exaggerated hand gestures
barely avoid spilled booze. Smokers
stand in circles about the sidewalk
flanking the door.

Why are you so self deprecating?

He means well. They always do, but
my humor flounders inversely to my salsa
heartbeat.

I don't belong.
I don't belong.

In the back of my head
incantations call the ghouls in me. Crawl
across my skin, behind my eyes,
nail my heels to a spot near the door and count
heads. When the smoke settles, when the last
stick is ashed, when one side of the blockade
turns its back a moment too long
I run.

I don't belong.
I don't belong.

Incantations carry me to bed, to black
sheets and a chill. How do you
convince yourself the sun isn't ashamed
to also touch you?

Have you stood in a room where the bass
shook the lines from the road outside and dozens of voices
sing stories to old strangers still

sound like a kind of love and somehow
all you hear is chanting?

I don't belong.
I don't belong.
They know it.
They know it.
They know I should be gone.
I should be gone.

Have you stood at the foot of a bed in a dark
room with only the muffled sound of the world
outside going on without you and somehow
all you hear is chanting?

I still don't belong.
Still.
Be still.

Confession #173:
Urge

Only once—middle lane mouth
bus terminal, between two sidewalk slopes,
hidden from the over-half moon judgment by
concrete and clouds—I screamed
to stop myself.

I could leave it there, bury all
my other thoughts in a million different graves, pray
no one sees the mud side of more
than one headstone.

Or here, in the white earth of this

I can place one truth atop the way
my toes stop a step before the edge
I feel the falling with my eyes
slipping story by story to the stop.

I don't dream of flying –

```
J     J     J
 u     u     u
  m     m     m
   p     p     p
J    J    J    J
 u    u    u    u
  m    m    m    m
   p    p    p    p
```

– or sometimes it is enough
to lightly step.

Confession #174:
Fear

a hundred pound heavy bag
hangs in the corner for those few nights
streetlights still slip through the yellowed venetian
engines and basses avoid the hour and the wolf
comes to my chest buries her
snout in my lungs cold and voracious my chest
heaves but I have no room to cry and under
my eyes I see the last black
where the wolf lives where
all the me the universe cares for will be and I
need to feel the canvas cut knuckles
deceitful yield of sand of earth of skin still
hoping to grow and refuse
to feed her this
gray this
thing between
ever black and only now
white these teeth I feel scraping
my air like pavement to chalk run
scraped knuckles down my cheek
breathe
breathe
breathe

Confession #175:
Honesty

Before you you read, please
stare at the white
until your mind clears, your eyes
stop fully believing, and answer me
honestly.

Do you know how hard it is to say
I am terrified to die
but sometimes
I sincerely want to?

Confession #333:
Rationalized

because I was tired
because I am less immune to stress than I think
because the night was cold and too full of voices
because sometimes the car is too far
because sometimes I just don't hear the phone
because sometimes I do hear the phone
because sometimes I wish I didn't
because I always wish I had
because I lie about being tired
because it isn't really tired the way you think,
       the way sleeping cures it
       the way I could wake up
       yawn all the tension in my back loose
       free my bare feet from the tangle of covers
       touch the hardwood floor and feel them
       ache for sun

Confession #8

I chant *Fuck Depression!*
And I almost think I could.

It's just the two of us alone in this bed
sharing skin beneath a dirty, black sheet.

Its hands touch me in all my most sensitive places,
wrapping me in itself like it needs me,

and I beg it   *love me*
even as it whispers, hot and breathy, in my ear:

I won't.
No one ever will.

Confession #463
God of Hunger

God of salivation
of oceans tossing tongues
of thunder in the hollowed trunks of men on their knees
of the claws primal beasts lay against the pit as they stir
of the blank mind
of the staggering steps to cold, white doors
of distention
of begging
of staring above empty palms
of never seeing them filled
of eyes that take the place of mouths
of mouths that take the place of sand
of mouths that take the place of other mouths
of mistaken emptiness
of aches of the flesh to drag the mind woefully back to emptiness,
be sated. Leave us to ignore our emptiness.
I hate you. I love you. I blaspheme and I can't
tell you which is heretical, but I plea,
tonight, and every darker night,
leave me without
ache for what simply will not.

Confession #756
Tempered

> *for S. Mantone*

Anger like the sharp end of an anvil
pressed against the right temple
a bass-blaster blacksmith
heavy metal hammer
scream-o until the skull bleeds each word
you'd rather keep inside

Confession #20

Words fail me. Beauty
is a thing for steady eyes,
single vision of assured perfection.
I speak of Pennsylvania's long 80.
I laugh at the 5 tunnels
between Pittsburgh and Philly.
I feel the bass rhythm
force my heart in sync. Maybe
the taste of tomorrow will be better
if the feel of tonight is this vague
blur of heartbeats and bodies.

Leave Confession #835 Alone

Harsh reds touch walls
around me.

Be the bull.

I do it and become
cliche.

The plastic strikes the ground. Disunity
and clatter.

It isn't always my blood.
We shouldn't want this.

Leave me my pain.
Let me inflict on the air
until there is nothing
to breathe.

Don't touch the raw hole
of this.
I bite when touched.
Even in tenderness.

I don't want to.

Confession #726:
Emotions and Men

This is not a lecture. This is a smile.
Read it by Braille and oak bark.
That will tell you as much about my heart
as a clock about how time moves
in nightmares.

Think I am one expression
at a time—I am always something else.
I am always everything
I can ever be.

Confession #660:
As a Man

I was probably wrong
when I spoke   about nerves and crowds
I gave it to anxiety
No   I need to be necessary

Point every eye at my smile and I will
twist   two-hundred plus   with the twitch of my lips
until the clock's hands tire
Sit me with six or seven sometimes
a dozen   beating chests   and I will be quietly
contented   to believe I belong
that I am at least wanted
        for a while

Make it a show of equals a mass of people
who could not care the distance of my body   and theirs
and I will shy to a cold corner
try   to be happy for those faces
that can beam

**Confession #661:
As a Man**

Necessity is likely a curse of masculinity.
Condemnation that we are worthless
if we are purposeless. The message being
almost always we are less
unless we can be kings.

I could be, but not by clawing or climbing.
I am the weakest of men. I cannot
claim in a crowd a spotlight or a glance.
I stand to the side and recite the silent prayer:

Please don't see me.
Please don't see me.

Just because I danced before does not mean
my body can move the same
with unfamiliar eyes.

Dance with anyone else.

Confession #662:
As a Man

I looked to my brothers and found them
by fives
setting down paper crowns
upon their ramparts

All these kings of cardboard castles
feigning all the success they are accused of having
reaching out to hold the air as they fall
believing a man is dust
if not an ogre king.

Confession #663:
As a Man

Can we please be broken
flawed
bleeding things

Please be damaged and dragging ourselves
still from mud

Please all be hurt and weep
together as equals in pain
none more than any other

Confession #664:
As a Man

It's too easy to say
something is gendered, sexed, beyond control; Why
I cry at night, sometimes,
about not belonging, about me
longing, about stupid bullshit I should quit
crying over.
I should just forget
my dark self. Stop leaving
my bravado face on the coat rack. Keep it on
overnight. Let the years graft its confidence to my skin,
seep its smile into my dreams, make me my public persona
privately, forget
that he is a lying me.

**Confession #79:
Response**

*But what is the greatest thing
a MAN should learn?*

You are not alone
in not knowing
what a *man* should be.

Your father, grandfather,
uncles, brothers, friends,
enemies, brief acquaintances
of your eyes and smiles
are all clueless of how to be
a *man*.

The more they insist,
the less they matter.

**Confession #80:
How to be a Man**

I insist I have no idea
how to be a man. I insist
I am one. Maybe
you are too.

I know how not to be
a man. I know what I do
to another body
will not make me more
a man.

I know what I do
to another body
could make me less.
Less man
by being less
human, less than human,
a beast consuming
blood or tears or unyielded flesh.

I do not know
how to be a man, but
I will not walk with wolves.

Confession #418:
Define a man

I.
And don't use his jaw   his stubble   the number of blades
he presses to his skin   and sometimes   bleeds   don't use
what bars he lifts   the knurl he grips   the tear of the callus
in the shape of the bar   the shape of the bottle   the shape of the air
early in an empty night as he opens his hand   closes his hand
                                                                                         opens his hand
don't use the size of his penis   the function of his penis   the presence
or form or bend or bow or any other part of a penis of this one percent of some
of our bodies so many mistakenly pack with a hundred percent of their pride
don't
use a body   don't use any   body
his body and his body and his body are not the same and so if we do if we use
any body to define every body then we will define too many bodies as other

II.
Tell me
what a man does. Tell me
what makes him
what he makes   what is made
because he
is a he
that could not be made by any
but him.

III.
And why is it always anger? Always
rage? Always
violence and violation and not
a cradle he could make with his arms   inviting the hurt to lay
                                                and weep
                                                and grow and sleep and
                                                leave
when the sky was more inviting
vacating the cradle
for the next in need to heal?

IV.
I have so little left
to say.   No,

that's not right,
what I have left is not
little. It is too large for my mouth.
It cannot fit
through the catch in my throat, cannot escape
these millions of bundled fruits grown in the dirt of my lungs
fed simmering blood and the stale air of this argument
about *who* and *how* and *why* and not   *why not*
every one of these hopeful words, these potential screams, remains
too rooted in my lungs.
If I push, I might pour the pulp from my chest, press it
until it is wine, parse it out to those who most need
to taste truth, be drunk
on a high proof embrace

V.
It is a small revolution to call yourself
a man
and allow anyone else the same
without comparison

**Confession #800:
Tell me where it hurts**

Like you have no sense of direction,
your fingers have never been compasses,
could never be
arrows fired singularly, but could be music
played in the dark between the moon and the air.

Like words only have meaning to your ears
and your tongue speaks ice and light
and daydreams of trout halfway through spawning.

Like you just found a rock
the shape of your childhood corner's,
the shape of the mini-mountain you scaled
before the bus arrived,
every morning, to feel big for a moment,
to have people look up their noses,
the shape of everything you've forgotten.

Tell me where it hurts
in any way that forgets the tears
unless you are building a new ocean
we can sail
to lands where ache has become a brick,
every salve become mortar, and
every man a mason.

Still Not Confession #835

Please, no. Please.

If I bury my pen beside the grey slate
slab atop the box that held the white and orange
body that was my cat my siblings and I
lowered reverently to rest along the wall
he freely strode beneath the grass
he laid in and I lose
my book between that old Lake George
back road where my first motorcycle ended and the street
Big Danny told his four-year-old to flee from in the dark
arms of her teenage mother before he took a bullet
for every year he spent loving her and the avenue
my biological father disappeared to the first time
he didn't want to be found then
maybe I can keep this one.

Maybe I can have one secret still my own.
We are creatures of secrets. I see the world lay bare
every thought as it happens and how much have we become
ourselves through committee instead of
ourselves through ourselves?

Confession #423:
Ode to Me

Two lips
Tulips
To lips
to sounds and not to touch
in fields of concrete flowers kilometers tall

Listen
and kiss me

You should want to

I speak life into glass
give it to the sun

Confession #50:
Debit

There is value
beyond mathematics, beyond bleeding
red or clotted black, beyond pale green
crinkling in a palm, the grip an infant has
on any passing body
anything to not be empty because it can't know
when it will touch again.

There is value in this
edge-worn plastic, this embossed rectangle
that holds my name, owns my name, is more me
than my skin.

And there is the value: more than me.
If I accept this, know this, lay my head
down with the moonlight drifting
behind thin clouds and write
its worth with the slivers of what shine remains
inside my eyelids, inside my skin,
will it hurt less? Will the ache in my shoulders pass?
Will the weight of emptiness slip from me
as emptiness should? Will I feel
worth?

Confession #3:
Beaten

I wanted to write like the beat
generation – Kerouac
Concision – Corso Commentary.

I wanted to shove my penis
into politics but the politicians beat
me to it, sans the figurative in
fucking. I had such desire

to rail against blather, but I'm not beat
like they were, not alive in societal
shit beholden to a definite,
declarative, unbroken spirit.

I am made of red-written
dollar signs – Olympus Mons
of Debt – and I swear
there's rumbling beneath; a buried beating
heart that, given another

millennium, might burst, blow
a chunk the size of the south
from the side. I'm not beat
like Ginsberg, screaming
for joy. I'm beat
like Baudelaire.

The could-be-dead volcano
would be my tomb, and generations
of children, not my own,
Crazyhorse my head into the rock with sticks
of dynamite and compressed
light and everyone who sees would ask
what I did to deserve my own
mountain monument and all
they will say is "This has everything
to do with desire stealing a face

owning on a speck of a rock in a space
on the other side of the sun
where it always comes to light but
people go blind looking for it."

Confession #567
How to Talk to a Liberal (if you must)
After Ann Coulter

Speak not as superior
Not as trainer to an unruly dog
Not as a person who has swam every drop of water,
      sung every note in the heavens,
      seen the face the future wears
      and know it as mirror.

Speak as change, the agent and the act
As ice in a palm, always water, but fluid in warmth
As the palm for thawing another

Confession #01/17

drift to the fogged edge
echoes of cheers feel in the bone
boots on spines and all the limbless forests
sway in that coral haze
coral dies
coral spray on holy sites
caustic glyphs and crowds
one-arm salutes
million-arm marches
walk to the morning
walk to the mourning
walk until it dawns
shift red
what is this
hand made of
my ribs stop short one beat
this breath of no time
who is this in my skin
who sees a clear tomorrow

Confession #02/17

fake thoughts sip tea inside me
mock this reality tv I'm living through
I know now I can't trust my eyes because
context lies and I might disagree
about p.c. making narcissists of a generation
or three but the snowflakes pile high on both seats
of this seesaw we strapped ourselves to and
why the Hell do these planks keep growing
who can see the bodies on the other end
this is the yelling before the wood splits and
fuck those guys
on the other side
because I must obviously be right
or left or maybe this sense of post-binary could be used
to mean I don't think in hard contrast
I live in fucked-up colors and we need these
hues and rainbows and steady tongues to see
bodies are bodies are bodies like ours and
there is no them
and and and and and
there is always more to say
until I haven't listened and
I hate this grander canyon of culture we keep
fracking until it rips us all in fours and fives
why can't this just be love
why can't this just be love
why can't this

Confession #5/24
Student Accommodations

I stand by the door on purpose. White
shirt, grey vest, spinning scissors
sometimes to fidget as I bash
Aristotle or talk evolution
cell to human to child to
corpse to numb   again as mothers
jump fences and names become numbers
higher than a single one's birthday and a student
asks me if I spin
scissors by the door for when a shooter walks in.
When a shooter walks in.
When.   I stand by the door
with a purpose and pretend it's protection,
like I imagine the barrel peeking in
and assessing,   evaluation day
you could never train for:

Do I have my class in order? In a row? Quiet,
Waiting,   silent as the dead?

Are my scores high enough to keep my students
alive? Standardized coffins, no accommodations, no
extra time to fill in the full circles with bullets
A through D through U*(valde)* through me

Please through me. Please. When you peak,
when   you stop by to see
which students will graduate
my class   (which way they leave)
please speak to me first.

I stand by the door on purpose,
to greet visitors, to ask to speak to them,
softly,   outside,   before
they have words with these students.
They're taking a test   always.
So leave them be
please,

just take me,   or   at least
make me first.
It's all the accommodation
I can promise.
They need extra
time.

**Confession #221:
Reading News**

a toddler passes
hand to hand
above razor wire

one family makes of themselves
nesting dolls
on train tracks
mother over infant
father over mother
billy clubs
over father

a sea of tents rises
falls with the flow
bodies and buckling spirits

the sea rises
falls with nothing atop
all the babes crashing
below

I lean back in my chair
drunken yelling in the street

This is my block
I was born here
You can leave or
I can take you out

fans drown them
with aid of sirens
I curl in my bed
the only lights are red
blue flashing
even the voice in my head
silent

Confession #5/28
What they are lying about

It keeps getting worse. The lies. The hiding. The 78 minutes
of decidedly dead air.

Lie about me. Say I tried. Say I died a hero with all the little ones
scattered at my feet.

Say it wasn't all the little ones. If you can, if you care, if you come
before the hour is up, maybe
the little ones won't have to lie about me.

Confession #835

This grave is freshly emptied. Roots
twist and twitch in the heavy air
lost without this body.

The bottom hasn't dried yet.
You can still feel the saltwater in the soil
through your fingers if you touch
words with your eyes half-closed.

This one is mine. Here I confess only
I am afraid
I will be splayed open too far to ever close
my heart will start beating air and voices
I've imagined whispering that schoolyard way

one hand touching the edges of lips
the edges of an ear
the breath like alchemy
murder in each recess syllable.

I will keep my secret
be whole in my rotting

Confession # -1
> *For Peter Kirn*

I tried to confess joy before Peter
hugged me farewell
reminded me that laughter is a vent
a pump to push the poison air from the soul.

He smelled vaguely of cabbage
and shit and unhindered sun and
that scent that comes just before you relearn
simplicity is the most complete contentment.

Thank You

This book was a labor in all the painful meanings of the word and all the ways it results in creation. There are so many people that need to be thanked and only so many pages to do it in, so forgive me if you do not see your name. I am limited here.

First, I must thank Finishing Line Press for seeing promise in this collection and giving it life outside of my computer. I owe much to these wonderful people. Support small presses and read other great poets from Finishing Line Press.

My fellow poets and inspirations: Yesenia Montilla, Roberto Carlos Garcia, Darla Himeles, Peter Kirn, Lynne McEniry, Michael Waters, Judith Vulmer, Ross Gay, Aracelis Girmay, Mihaela Moscaliuc, Anne Marie Macari, and a dozen plus other amazing people that help keep me inspired.

I have to especially thank Mike Bross and A.E. Bross for putting up with me, reading my work, and giving me regular feedback. Tanya Voytus needs a special thank you for the amazing artwork done for the cover. Thanks to Michelle Oats for the years of friendship and support through some of our toughest days. And as always, absolutely no thanks goes to Michelle Greco.

Finally, to my many family members (quite a few who are named throughout this) I need to thank you and deeply apologize for all of this. Hopefully, none of you but the early readers, Justin Christopher, Ryan Lazar, and Elif Onursal-Dwyer will ever read this or any of these poems, otherwise I might have a lot of explaining to do. My life has actually been quite privileged and filled with joy because my mother, Tayo Euston, never let her children feel the lean or the uncertain times. Nobody else in the world has been there for me as long, as consistently, or as genuinely. Thank you for all of your sacrifices and the lives you let us all build.

Fletch Fletcher is a poet (obviously), a science teacher, a brother, and a bunch of other random things that may or may not help you understand him. He was lucky enough to work with and learn from amazing poets while getting an MFA in Poetry at Drew University. Fletcher's first collection, *Existing Science* (2021), was published by Assure Press.

www.ingramcontent.com/pod-product-compliance
Lightning Source LLC
Chambersburg PA
CBHW020338170426
43200CB00006B/428